Praise for
Dreams to Action Trailblazer's Guide

Dr. Julie Connor's book is thought-provoking and insightful as you pursue your dreams. It is laid out like a guidebook to take you from point A to point B with grace and ease. I encourage you to take the next step on your journey and move your dreams to action.

- Dr. Michelle Robin
author of *The E Factor: Engage, Energize, Enrich* and *Wellness on a Shoestring*

Dr. Julie Connor redefined goal setting and built a "dream-setting" framework that is pragmatic, easy to follow, and extremely comprehensive. The steps she takes you through will open your heart, your mind, and your soul to the dreams that live within you. Through her innovative tactics, you will not only have the tools to give birth to your dreams, but envision them like never before!

- Rebekah Radice
social media & content marketing expert/ consultant/speaker/trainer, Los Angeles, CA

Dreams to Action Trailblazer's Guide distills the process of creating a soul-satisfying and fulfilling life into accessible, approachable steps. If you follow the roadmap developed through Julie's own inspiring journey, expect to be enlivened and transformed!

- Dr. Christy L. Johnson
Intuitive Heal LLC, Williston, VT

Dr. Julie Connor's work is dedicated to helping people clearly define their dreams, identify their resources, and discover the means to uncovering their greatness. Read and apply the wisdom contained in *Dreams to Action Trailblazer's Guide* – you will be given a clear road map to envisioning and manifesting your destiny. You will be glad you did.

- Brian K. Knight
host of *Success Profiles Radio*, Chandler, AZ

This book is a must if you are looking to achieve your dreams. Everything is explained step-by-step, easy to understand, and apply. When I started reading it, I couldn't stop until the end. I am astounded by all the amazing keys that Dr. Julie Connor is giving us.

- Carèle Bélanger
social media specialist, Montreal, Canada

Dreams to Action Trailblazer's Guide is a must-have book, for anyone looking for some precise direction to putting their thoughts to action. In order to realize their goals and dreams, they must blaze a trail for themselves to be a blessing to others.

- Lynda Coleman
artist/poetpreneur/trailblazer, Austin, TX

Dr. Connor writes, "Passion fuels dreams. Commitment fuels action." The book is more than thought-provoking; it challenges you to act on your goals to reach your dreams. It encourages you to write it down and makes sure you do something about it.

- Kei San Pablo
The K Squad Outsourcing Solutions, Manila, Philippines

Praise for
Dreams to Action **Trailblazer's Guide**

I learned a lot from Julie's experiences. I am going through similar changes in my life now. Dr. Connor truly inspired me to keep focusing on my dream, plan, and bring it into real actions. I hope to go back to the *Dreams to Action Trailblazer's Guide* many times in the future as a reminder for me to focus in my dream.

> - Chitra Poudel
> engineer, Lee's Summit, MO

Sometimes, there seems to be a gulf between where we are and where we want to be. Dr. Julie Connor brings these worlds together in her aptly titled *Dreams to Action Trailblazer's Guide*. She takes you by the hand and empowers you to soar beyond your excuses and perceived limitations. This book is a COMPULSORY companion for anyone who is sick and tired of "average."

> - John Obidi
> social media strategist, Benin, Nigeria

Dreams to Action Trailblazer's Guide shows how planning and taking action shape our dream lives into our daily lives. Dr. Julie's book is an immersive 3-D experience. It is a must-read, must-implement, thought-provoking, thought-implementing guide to experiencing the life your inner being desires.

> - Nathan W. Pace
> personal life coach, New Harmony, UT

I am a visionary, a dreamer, a man of prayer. I just finished *Dreams to Action Trailblazer's Guide* by Dr. Julie Connor. The good news: I really enjoyed the book. The bad news: I have work to do! Thank you.

> - Dr. Robert Sexauer, Clinton, MO

As I read this book, I relaxed and reflected on my dream. I actually loved doing the work and started feeling more hopeful and successful within a few exercises. I was totally hooked and will continue to practice these principles from here on out!

> - Scott Merian
> Merian Financial Services, Berkley, MI

Dreams to Action Trailblazer's Guide offers an amazing and easy step-by-step plan that anyone can do in order to achieve their life or business goals. Thank you, Dr. Julie Connor, for being such an inspiration! Go, Trailblazers!!

> - Tamara Graham
> interior decorator, Toronto, Canada

Dr. Connor's guide is clear and the concepts are easy to grasp; I can use her goal-setting tips for personal growth and as a trainer and instructor. My brain is firing with new ideas!

> - Monique McDaniel
> fitness instructor & trainer, Kansas City, MO

Dr. Julie Connor
LIGHT YOUR PASSION

Dreams to Action Trailblazer's Guide

How to Transform Your Dream into Reality

Dr. Julie Connor

www.DrJulieConnor.com

TABLE OF CONTENTS

TABLE OF CONTENTS

ACKNOWLEDGEMENTS

The *Dreams to Action Trailblazer's Guide* is dedicated to bold trailblazers who believe there is an Unlimited Power within them where all things are possible. To all of those who courageously step into their dreams with hope, passion, purpose, and daring conviction, this book was written for you.

I am indebted to Nancy Oglesby who ruthlessly edited the final copy of this book and provided meticulous feedback. I owe heartfelt thanks to Teresa Carnes and Lori Snow at Point Graphics for sharing their creative genius with me in the design and layout of this book. I am thankful for the collective wisdom and support from Rose Tubati, Allen Clayton, and members of our mastermind group. I am grateful to Rev. William Walter, C.PP.S, who is a model of collaborative leadership and Jon Schuley for his inspirational influence. I wish to thank Beth McWilliams Stone, a high school friend who tirelessly connects graduates from Jennings Senior High School and, in her gentle way, inspires others to embrace their own light. I am grateful to Mary Kay Stashefsky for her lifelong friendship and boundless encouragement. Words do not adequately express my admiration and infinite gratitude to my mentor and friend, Elizabeth Heidler, who embodies all of the character traits I value and want to emulate in my own journey. And, most especially, to Patrick Dougherty, whose words, "Don't Ever Give Up," is in the center of my vision board and whose love is at the core of my heart.

Always remember there are only two kinds of people in this world – the realists and the visionaries. The realists know where they're going. The visionaries have already been there.

– Robert Orben

INTRODUCTION

If your life was a book, what would you want people to remember about your story?

Embracing your life with passion requires imagination to dream, courage to boldly leap into the unknown, commitment to a vision, and faith that trusts in the abundant potential within you where all things are possible. As a professional speaker, writer, teacher, and consultant, I show others how to define their purpose, align their vision with their core values, maximize their talents, and create tangible goals.

Throughout the last three decades, I invited adults and students, churches and schools, nonprofit organizations and businesses into exciting, gritty, and sometimes difficult challenges of authentic dialogue and collaborative planning. The processes I used to introduce goal-setting strategies were dramatically altered after I mistakenly used the wrong word during a conversation with high school students. I meant to ask a student, "What is your *goal*?" However, the question that tumbled out of my mouth was "What is your *dream?*"

His classmates stopped talking to listen to his response.

"I don't know," he admitted. "No one's ever asked me that question before."

How was it possible that I shared so many practical resources designed to help others reach *extrinsic* goals without showing them how to use those tools to pursue *intrinsic* desires? Planners and calendars are designed to organize activities in ways that help us complete tasks – tasks that are often attached to someone else's goal. When we use these tools without awareness of our own aspirations or claim to our own dreams, we become dependent on others to point us in the right direction. Goals without a dream are like arrows without a target.

What is *your* dream?

You will find the answer to this question – and discover how to (1) define your dream, (2) create a plan and chart your course, and (3) take action – within your responses on the pages of the *Dreams to Action Trailblazer's Guide.*

Buckle up.

DREAM BIG! IT'S IMPORTANT

Children eagerly describe their dreams, but this question causes many adults to scratch their heads. When we were young, our choices were driven by what felt fun and exciting. Children often grow into adults who swap dreams for responsible decisions and, over time, forget what made them feel alive with passionate purpose and joy.

Kristoffer Howes, search engine marketing and brand strategist, stated, "A dream is the visualization of your goal and the motivation for your soul." There is good logic supporting the old adage, "Seeing is believing." More than 2,000 years ago, Aristotle advised his students, "First, have a definite, clear, practical ideal – a goal, an objective. Second, have the necessary means to achieve your ends – wisdom, money, materials, and methods. Third, adjust all your means to that end."

Getting Started

I received a letter from a school district where I worked as an instructional coach shortly after completing my dissertation. It outlined reductions in staff. My services were no longer needed.

Several years earlier, I entered graduate school with a hungry desire to leap out of traditional educational positions into a career I loved. However, I had no words to describe "a career I loved." I felt anxious and afraid as I looked into my uncertain future, but I intuitively recognized this was my opportunity to move from what was familiar into what I was created to do: I wanted to inspire others.

When I was a youth minister at a small church in a college community twenty years ago, I belonged to a collaborative staff that was committed to shared decision-making practices. Throughout one grueling summer, we created vision and mission statements that mirrored our core values. We outlined goals aligned with our vision and mission. I used the same tools to develop goals with my religious education team and youth leadership council.

I received many invitations from churches and schools to present vision, mission, collaboration, and goal-setting strategy workshops. Every time I facilitated meaningful dialogue in ways that allowed others to define their purpose and create tangible goals, I heard a voice within me sing, "I want this to be the primary focus of my career for the rest of my life!" But I did not believe I had the time, knowledge, resources, or connections to act upon the intuitive desire to step into my passion. So, I stopped thinking about it. For twenty years.

I engaged in collaborative dialogue with teachers and school administrators as an instructional coach, but conversations were usually confined to analyses of common and formal testing data. District downsizing provided me with a spectacular opportunity to step out on my own and design workshops that helped groups mold nebulous ideas into concrete statements of purpose.

As an independent speaker and consultant, I was unsure how to take meaningful planning and goal-setting tools to a larger audience. I had to do more than *think about* how to move forward, I had to *do something*. Throughout the challenging months that followed, I shaped my dream into a solid purpose statement. I defined specific steps with manageable goals that made me feel excited when I read them. I crafted a personal plan of action. The discovery process led to the contents within this book.

Do You Have a Dream?

You will find valuable information within the *Dreams to Action Trailblazer's Guide* if any of the following questions resonate within you:

- Do you want to discover your dream?
- Do you have a dream, but question if it can come true?
- Do you have a dream, but wonder if you have the knowledge or skills to transform it into a reality?
- Do you have a dream, but do not know how to create a plan?
- Do you have a dream, but do not know if you have time to pursue it?
- Do you have a dream, but doubt whether you have the resources or support necessary to pursue your passion?

If your response is "yes" to any of these questions, let's start this journey together.

When you plan a trip, you make preparations before you leave your home. You choose a destination and find time within your calendar to go on your trip. You purchase tickets and make travel arrangements. You pack clothing that is appropriate for the climate of your destination. You make decisions to manage responsibilities that must be handled in your absence.

However, if you discovered there was going to be a four-hour boarding delay at your gate at the airport on the day you planned to take your vacation, would you get on a different plane that was scheduled at your time of departure without learning more information about the destination? Faster is not always better. The twists and turns along the journey to your dream destination hold the information and experiences you need to keep you on course.

What is your dream destination? If you were in an airplane that was chartered to take you wherever you wanted to go with all of the ideal upgrades and advantages you could possibly imagine, where would your airplane land? Your responses to these questions will help you chart a course that will lead you to success.

Access Your Power

"Why do I have to write anything?" asked a gentleman at one of my goal-setting workshops. He flipped through the pages of the printed resources. "This looks like a lot of work. I just want to do what I want to do."

"What do you want to do?" I asked.

"Well," he replied, "it's complicated."

Lee Iacocca, former Chrysler CEO and author of *Iacocca: An Autobiography*, explained, "The discipline of writing something down is the first step toward making it happen." When you commit to your dream and make a decision to pursue your passion, you must use both parts of your brain to reach your goals.

As you define your goals and develop systems of efficient time management, you access your logical left brain. When you imagine and clearly articulate your goals *in writing*, you access the creative energy of your right brain. Imagination and creativity allow you to find solutions to problems that were not previously available to you and give your left brain an opportunity to be receptive to new ideas.

"All things are created twice. There's a mental or first creation and a physical or second creation of all things," added Stephen Covey, author of *The 7 Habits of Highly Effective People.* "You have to make sure the blueprint, the first creation, is really what you want, that you've thought everything through." He maintained that the "blueprint" of our dreams provide the creative framework that allow us to "begin with the end in mind" when we chart our course.

Let's start this journey with a dreaming exercise. Be specific. Use strong describing words that allow you to experience what it is like to step into your dream destination.

Affirm What You Want

What would I like to **BE**?

_____

_____

_____

_____

_____

_____

_____

_____

What would I like to **DO**?

_____

_____

_____

_____

_____

What would I like to **EXPERIENCE**?

_____

_____

_____

_____

_____

_____

_____

_____

Why is what I want to **BE, DO,** and **EXPERIENCE** important to me?

_____

_____

_____

_____

_____

_____

_____

_____

To create a plan that leads to what you want to be, do, or experience, you must acknowledge your current location so you can chart a course of action.

dream
dream
dream

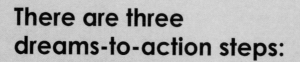

There are three dreams-to-action steps:

Dream It   Identify and describe your dream with precise, razor-sharp clarity.

Plan It   Create a course of action that streamlines your schedule and maximizes your time to engage in goal-related activities.

Do It   Honor your commitment to yourself and to your dream by boldly taking action.

Your responses to the following questions will help you articulate your dream:

What did I love to do as a child?

_____

_____

_____

_____

_____

_____

What most excites me?

_____

_____

_____

_____

_____

_____

_____

What makes me feel the most angry or upset?

_____

_____

_____

_____

_____

Our emotions, like our words, contain power.

How can I use what most excites, angers, or upsets me to achieve what I want to be, do, or experience?

_____

_____

_____

_____

_____

_____

_____

_____

_____

_____

Define Your Dream

Michael Gerber, author of *Awakening the Entrepreneur Within*, describes a dream as "a statement of the greater good you want to create in the world." He explains that a dream "allows us to commit ourselves to something that has meaning, something that moves us, that inspires us, that awakens our passion."

In *Put Your Dream to the Test*, John C. Maxwell adds that a dream is "an inspiring picture of the future that energizes your mind, will, and emotions, empowering you to do everything you can to achieve it." As you think about all of the exciting possibilities connected to your dream, consider:

- Do you want to fully experience your brilliant potential?
- Is living in alignment with your core values important to you?
- Are you ready to use your gifts to make a difference in the world?

In this part of the dreams-to-action process, do not worry whether or not your dream is realistic, affordable, or achievable. Defining manageable goals is crucial, but not during this dreaming phase. This part of the process invites guidance from your imagination. Important questions to consider during the dreaming stage include:

What is my dream?

_____
_____
_____
_____
_____
_____
_____

Why is my dream important to me?

_____
_____
_____

_____
_____
_____
_____

How do I feel when I think about my dream?

_____
_____
_____
_____
_____
_____

How does my dream bring good into the lives of other people?

_____
_____
_____
_____
_____
_____
_____
_____

When you dream, you explore new solutions you would not ordinarily consider and think about new possibilities. Do not worry about how you must orchestrate events to ensure your success. Focus instead on *why* your dream is important to you. When you can *define* your dream and articulate *why* you want to pursue it, answers about *how* to do it will begin to become clear.

Design a Vision Board

Sometimes it is difficult to articulate your dream if you forgot what you enjoy. One way to watch your dream take shape is through creation of a vision board.

Mike Dooley, author of *Leveraging the Universe: 7 Steps to Engaging Life's Magic*, insists, "Our positive thoughts are at least 10,000 times more powerful than our negative thoughts." When you create a vision board, you gather a vivid collection of images and words that mirror your preferences, passions, and goals. As you surround yourself with inspiring words and images, you welcome new ideas and exciting possibilities into your life. This process invites positive change and opportunities into your subconscious mind.

I created a vision board shortly after I left my last position as an instructional coach. I no longer wanted to work in traditional school settings, but I had no idea what I wanted to do next.

I flipped through pages of magazines to find pictures and stories that made me feel motivated and joyful. I found meaningful quotations and inspiring words. I purchased a sheet of poster paper and attached my collection of pictures and words to its surface. It became my vision board. I slowly rediscovered what made my heart dance: one word, one photo, one phrase, one conversation, one motivating quotation, one goal, one habit, one change, one risk at a time.

Vision Board Creation Process

Materials for creating a vision board include poster paper, glue, scissors, magazines, and newspapers. You can also use paint, magic markers, stickers, photographs, and clippings from the Internet. I purchased a large white foam display board (similar to exhibit boards used for science fair projects). The tri-fold structure allows for convenient display in a place at home where I often see it. I bought a glue stick with nonpermanent adhesive; it permits me to attach or remove objects on my vision board.

Find time for quiet reflection before you search for **VISION BOARD** pictures and phrases. Look back at your previous responses to questions in this book and consider:

- What is your dream?
- Where would you like to go?
- Who do you want to invite into your life?
- What new habits do you want to adopt?
- What new opportunities would you like to see come into your experience?

Create A Vision Board

Step 1: **Leaf through magazines and newspapers.** Scroll through Internet resources. Pay attention to words and images that appeal to you and align with things you want to experience.

Step 2: **Decide which goal or intention is most important for you.** Place images associated with this goal in a prominent position at the center of your vision board.

Step 3: **Group similar images and words into clusters on your vision board.** Dispose of images that do not make you feel energized and excited. Adjust your selections until you are comfortable with each item's placement.

Step 4: **Adhere all of the items to the surface of the board.**

Step 5: **Display your vision board in a place where you will see it.**

Your vision board is a work in progress; therefore, you will probably not complete it in one sitting. A vision board will change and grow as you change and grow. Remove items that reflect goals you reached or no longer capture your interest. Replace them with new selections. As you open your heart to more opportunities, you experience greater motivation to try new things and greater enthusiasm about living your own life.

Dream Clarity

How can you more clearly articulate your dream?

Try these steps:

- **Allow time for quiet reflection.** Be open to inspiration and direction by visualizing the experience of achieving your dream at the beginning of every day. Invite gentle guidance to influence your words, actions, and choices throughout the day.

- **Brainstorm.** Keep a small notebook with you to record ideas that come to you throughout the day. Ask other people about their dreams. Engage in conversations with people you trust about your dreams. Listen. Share. Discover new ideas.

- **Conduct research.** Read. "Dream surf" on the Internet and peruse subject areas that arouse your interest. Network with individuals who share similar dreams and transform their aspirations into careers, hobbies, or positive lifestyle changes. Join Internet communities to meet people and exchange ideas with those who share your passions.

- **Practice.** Cultivate your gifts and talents. Take lessons. Enroll in classes. Engage in activities where you can hone your skills in a nurturing environment.

- **Stay motivated.** Post pictures of role models in places where you will frequently see them. Read inspirational material that encourages you to pursue your passions.

- **Create affirmations.** Positive affirmations allow you to focus deliberate intention on desired outcomes. Affirmations are always stated in present tense; they are personal and specific. A statement such as "I ignore self-doubting thoughts and won't focus on negative outcomes" invites self-doubt, lack of focus, and negative outcomes. A constructive affirmation such as "Fabulous ideas flow to me in a river of abundance" invites creative ideas and inspiration. You will learn more about affirmations in the last chapter, *Do It! Kick It into Gear.*

- **Start a gratitude journal.** My life dramatically changed when I committed to a daily writing practice of recording experiences that filled me with appreciation for good things in my life. A grateful spirit positively shifts your attitude and adjusts your perspective. Through an optimistic daily writing practice, your dreams reintroduce themselves to you and invite positive expectation into your life.

These activities encourage you to trust in your own ability to make good decisions. The more you become intentionally aware of and nurture your unique gifts and talents, the more confidence you discover within you and the more receptive you become to the flow of positive experiences into your life.

Dream Clarity

- Allow Time for Quiet Reflection
- Brainstorm
- Conduct Research
- Practice
- Stay Motivated
- Create Affirmations
- Start a Gratitude Journal

DREAM IT! YOUR ROLES AND RESPONSIBILITIES

Your passion is your internal compass that will guide you towards your dreams and future goals. We walked through several steps in the previous chapter to help you describe your dream. Once you define your dream, how do you get from where you are to where you want to go?

Charging Forward

I wanted to experience something new and exciting after I left my previous position in an urban school district. At the time, I did not have the words to articulate my destination. I repeatedly applied for teaching and school administration positions, even though I did not want to teach in an elementary or secondary school or be a school administrator. The application process for those positions was familiar.

Creation of a vision board and journaling helped me clarify my preferences, develop new ideas, and identify new goals. Participation in activities listed in the previous chapter helped me embrace my personal gifts and talents, stirred my passions, and allowed me to welcome positive change into my life.

I took acting classes, but discovered I was no longer interested in theater as a performer. I volunteered to sing at church, but I preferred to sit next to my fiancé during services. Exploration and experimentation helped me distinguish exhilarating activities from interests that no longer appealed to me.

My dreams of becoming a professional speaker and writer had not disappeared. They were always with me. Years ago, I was too frightened to pursue my dreams because I did not believe they could come true. So, my dreams took a nap until I woke up.

This was not a venture I could pursue without a source of income. While I carved out a new future,

I also worked in an office as an administrative assistant. I edited research. I was an adjunct instructor at area colleges. I provided in-service workshops to school districts. I struggled to find balance as I constructed a new career. The most difficult step was the decision to start somewhere and do something.

"Vulnerability sounds like truth and feels like courage," explains Brené Brown, author of *Daring Greatly*. "Vulnerability is our most accurate measurement of courage." She describes the place of embracing our fear and owning our power as "stepping into the arena." Scripture calls it "holy ground" (Exodus 3:5). I call it spectacular.

As an employee of other organizations, I did not worry about marketing myself because providing presentations and workshops for specific audiences was part of my job. Speaking engagements were arranged within other departments where I worked. I had to figure out how to manage all of the moving parts and responsibilities when I decided to form my own company.

The thought of developing a plan to become a professional speaker and writer was terrifying and overwhelming. My fears and apprehensions were enormous – at first. Past experiences taught me to make a choice and take one step forward. I learned how to build my own website at DrJulieConnor. com and started a blog. I joined Toastmasters. I joined the National Speakers Association. I contacted others who shared my interests and introduced myself at networking events. I submitted articles that appeared in professional journals. I volunteered to do free workshops with at-risk youth and families. My daily consistent efforts gradually resulted in referrals and paid invitations to speak to larger groups.

Paulo Coelho, author of *The Alchemist*, states, "There is only one thing that makes a dream impossible to achieve: the fear of failure." Rebekah Radice, social media strategist and digital marketing specialist, encourages you to stop dwelling on obstacles and focus instead on your dream. She explains, "It's all about mindset. Once you change your mindset and recognize your value, doors of opportunity begin to open."

How Many Hats Do You Wear?

Your wear many "hats" and step into different roles as you juggle various responsibilities throughout your day. Your "hats" (or roles) may include "student," "parent," "spouse," "caregiver," "friend," "coach," "employee," "employer," or "volunteer." Managing multiple roles can be stressful, but understanding your roles provides you with vital information as you prioritize your time and involvement in various activities.

Describe your most important roles. Include "innovator," "visionary," or "dreamer" as one of your roles because it allows you to be open to all sorts of possibilities.

Role:_____

_____

_____

_____

_____

Role:_____

_____

_____

_____

_____

Role:_____

_____

_____

_____

_____

Role:_____

_____

_____

_____

_____

Role:_____

_____

_____

_____

_____

Role:_____

_____

_____

_____

_____

Role:_____

_____

_____

_____

_____

Your Roles and Your Future

Think about what you would like to do *three to five years from now*. What roles would you like to step into? What are you doing in these roles? Where are you doing it? Who shares responsibilities with you? Who is affected by your decisions?

Roles change with time, especially as we look with anticipation into the future. For example, your role as "employee" in the last exercise may be "employer" in this exercise.

Be specific. Describe your roles in *present* tense. You may write something like, "I manage a marketing office with *50 or more* employees." Use numbers in ways that reflect openness to incredible possibilities. If you add *"or more"* to a potential number or amount as described in the example, you do not set limits within your roles. Imagine and enjoy all of the wonderful opportunities that await you.

Role:_____
_____
_____
_____
_____

Role:_____
_____
_____
_____
_____

Role:_____
_____
_____
_____
_____

Role:_____
_____
_____
_____

Role:_____
_____
_____
_____

Role:_____
_____
_____
_____

Role:_____
_____
_____
_____

Your Roles and Positive Action Steps

How can you use the knowledge and skills you *have* to acquire the knowledge and skills you *want?* What can you do *today* that will prepare you for future roles? Describe positive action steps that will equip you with the knowledge and skills you will need for future roles in the spaces listed below.

Although you are a "student" or "home manager" at this time, you may desire to be a "chef" who specializes in Indian cuisine. You need not wait five years to pursue your passion; start today. You might write as an action step, "I find a new recipe for an Indian entrée and serve it to my family this week."

Be specific. Write your response in *present tense.* Your answers will allow you to see how you can make empowering decisions *today* that positively affect the direction of your life.

Role or Future Role: _____

_____

Action Step: _____

_____
_____
_____
_____
_____

Role or Future Role: _____

_____

Action Step: _____

_____
_____
_____
_____
_____

Role or Future Role: _____

_____

Action Step: _____

_____
_____
_____
_____

Role or Future Role: _____

_____

Action Step: _____

_____
_____
_____
_____
_____

Role or Future Role: _____

_____

Action Step: _____

_____

_____

_____

_____

_____

_____

Role or Future Role: _____

_____

Action Step: _____

_____

_____

_____

_____

_____

_____

Your Skills and Knowledge Chart

Consider the knowledge and talents you presently possess. Use the MY SKILLS AND KNOWLEDGE CHART to (1) acknowledge gifts and talents you possess and (2) list skills and information that will successfully help you to complete tasks associated with roles that you want to experience in the future.

A condensed version that includes some of my skills and talents are provided in this chart example. A copy of MY SKILLS AND KNOWLEDGE CHART for your use can be found in the appendix of this book.

MY SKILLS AND KNOWLEDGE CHART

SKILLS I Have	SKILLS I Want
Graphic arts skills	Website design skills
Video presentation skills	Video recording skills
KNOWLEDGE I Have	**KNOWLEDGE I Want**
English language mastery	Spanish language proficiency
Research writing expertise	Novel writing expertise

Understanding the skills and responsibilities tied to each of your roles and activities with which you engage today will empower you with the confidence needed to move steadily in the direction of your dreams.

DREAM IT! YOUR VISION AND MISSION

Why Vision and Mission Statements are Invaluable

Clearly articulated vision and mission statements reflect your beliefs and core values. They become the standard by which you measure everything in your life. Your personal vision and mission guide the words you speak, decisions you make, goals you create, and events you include into your daily schedule.

When I meet with groups to create organizational vision and mission statements, it is not uncommon for some participants to protest, "Is this really necessary?" They often want to charge into the day's immediate duties and responsibilities. Tasks without purpose often result in pointless discussions and unnecessary activities if they are not aligned with goals. When our goals flow from our mission and vision statements, we are free to select activities that align with our core values and purpose. We are less likely to waste our own time.

Your core values are at the center of who you are and how you want to be perceived by others. Mahatma Gandhi said, "Your beliefs become your thoughts. Your thoughts become your words. Your words become your actions. Your actions become your habits. Your habits become your values. Your values become your destiny." Your core values are tested through your words, actions, and the decisions you make each day.

A vision statement articulates the big idea of *who you are* and *what* you are working towards as a goal. It expresses *how* you want to be perceived and the legacy you want to share with others. It is an expression of your core values. Your vision reflects your dream; it is a picture of the future you would like to create. It should be concise and easy to remember.

Listed below are examples of meaningful vision statements:

- *CSX Corporation:* Our vision is to be the safest, most progressive North American railroad, relentless in the pursuit of customer and employee excellence.

- *Heifer International:* The vision of Heifer International is a world of communities living together in peace and equitably sharing the resources of a healthy planet.

- *Kauffman Foundation:* Our vision is to foster a society of economically independent individuals who are engaged citizens in their communities.

A **mission statement** is an action statement that reflects your vision. It clarifies (1) *what* you want to do, (2) *who* you do it for, and (3) *how* you do what you do. It is a broad declaration of your purpose that distinguishes you from others. It is an expression of how you hope to transform your dream into reality.

Examples of strong mission statements include the following:

- *American Red Cross:* The American Red Cross prevents and alleviates human suffering in the face of emergencies by mobilizing the power of volunteers and the generosity of donors.

- *San Diego Zoo Global:* The San Diego Zoo Global is committed to saving species worldwide by uniting our expertise in animal care and conservation science with our dedication to inspiring passion for nature.

- The *Julliard School:* The mission of The Julliard School is to provide the highest caliber of artistic education for gifted musicians, dancers, and actors from around the world so that they may achieve their fullest potential as artists, leaders, and global citizens.

Listed below are my vision and mission statements:

- *My Vision Statement:* I inspire people everywhere to pursue their dreams with confident passion.

- *My Mission Statement:* I provide others with the knowledge and tools needed to transform their dream into a plan of action.

Stephen Covey insisted that vision and mission statements are "more powerful, more significant, more influential than the baggage of the past or even the accumulated noise of the present." Strong vision and mission statements ground us with purpose and provide us with clear direction.

Create a Personal Vision Statement

A **vision statement** empowers you by focusing attention on your dream and desired results. Your vision creates a mental picture of your goal and becomes a source of inspiration and commitment for the future. It provides meaning to every task you want to accomplish and becomes the driving force behind your goals.

How would I describe myself to someone? Be specific. Write your response in *present* tense.

_____

_____

_____

_____

_____

_____

_____

What do I believe? _____

_____

_____

_____

_____

_____

_____

What do I want to offer to others? _____

_____

_____

_____

_____

_____

_____

What can I do to improve the lives of others?

_____

_____

_____

_____

_____

_____

Meaningful Vision Statement Questions

"A vision is a mental picture about what tomorrow will look like," explain James Kouzes and Barry Posner, authors of *The Leadership Challenge*. "It sets us apart and makes us feel special." Consider your responses to these questions as you think about your vision statement:

- Does my vision statement express how I want to be perceived by others?
- Does it convey my purpose?
- Does it represent what I think is possible?
- Does it point to my future?
- Does it reflect my core values?
- Does it express my strengths and unique capabilities?
- Do I feel inspired and motivated when I read or say it?

Write a Draft of Your Vision Statement

Use the information from your responses to create a vision statement draft. Keep it simple; no more than one or two sentences are necessary. A powerful vision statement contains two precise elements. It describes (1) your unique identity or purpose for your future and it is (2) an expression of your core values.

_____

_____

_____

_____

_____

_____

_____

_____

Compose a Powerhouse Mission Statement

As you consider a personal **mission statement**, Stephen Covey suggested, "Begin with the end in mind." A strong mission statement describes (1) *what* you want to do, (2) *who* you do it for, and (3) *how* you do what you do. It is composed in *present* tense and summarizes how you plan to execute your vision. As you think about your mission statement, consider these questions:

What do I want people to say about me at my funeral? _____

_____

_____

_____

_____

_____

_____

What lifetime accomplishments do I want people to remember? _____

_____

_____

_____

_____

_____

What can I do that adds value to my life and value to the lives of others? _____

_____

_____

_____

_____

_____

What values and principles do I admire in others?

_____

_____

_____

_____

_____

What values and principles are important to me?

_____

_____

_____

_____

_____

_____

_____

_____

What are my talents? _____

_____

_____

_____

_____

_____

_____

_____

How do I use my talents in my various roles?

_____

_____

_____

_____

_____

_____

Write a Draft of Your Mission Statement

Now it is time to begin a draft of your mission statement. It is an action statement that reflects your vision and core values. Remember to be specific and to keep it simple. Write your mission statement in *present* tense. Your mission statement articulates (1) *what* you want to do, (2) *who* you do it for, and (3) *how* you do what you do.

_____

_____

_____

_____

_____

_____

_____

_____

_____

Meaningful vision and mission statements serve as your directional compass. You do not need standards or principles dictated by someone else; you are grounded in your own sense of purpose and core values. As you align your words, thoughts, and actions with your vision and mission statements, you possess a clear lens through which you choose to view the world.

Assess Your Vision and Mission Statements

Creation of personal vision and mission statements is not an instantaneous endeavor. The composition process typically requires deep introspection and thoughtful revisions before they reach their final form. Periodic review of your vision and mission statements realigns you with your dream and core values. When you assess your vision and mission statements, keep in mind the following questions:

How do my vision and mission statements reflect who I am and what I want to share with the world?

_____
_____
_____
_____
_____
_____
_____
_____
_____

How are my core values reflected in what I want to accomplish within these statements?

_____
_____
_____
_____
_____
_____
_____
_____
_____

"All successful men and women are big dreamers," explains Brian Tracy, author of *Eat That Frog! 21 Ways Great Ways to Stop Procrastinating and Get More Done in Less Time.* "They imagine what their future could be, ideal in every respect, and then they work every day toward their distant vision, that goal or purpose." Tracy maintains you experience success by design, not by chance. Your willingness to make decisions, plan, and take action determines the course of your life. Your vision and mission statements provide a firm foundation for developing powerful goals.

Clearly articulated goals aligned with your vision and mission statements motivate you and galvanize your efforts to move forward towards your dream. We will explore ways you can successfully create meaningful goals in the next chapter, *Plan It! Define Your Goals.*

PLAN IT! DEFINE YOUR GOALS

Envision Your Lifetime Goals

A "bucket list" is a phrase that dates back to the 1700s and refers to all of the things you would like to do before you "kick the bucket" (or before the end of your life). The exciting part about this activity is that it invites you to tune into the power of your imagination. Focus on wonderful experiences that excite, motivate, and inspire you.

As we discussed in the first chapter, *Dream Big! It's Important*, the process that guides you from where you are to your dream destination encourages cooperation between your logical left brain and your creative right brain. When you imagine and clearly articulate your goals *in writing*, you access the creative energy of your right brain.

Use the spaces below to write very specific statements about events you would like to experience throughout your lifetime. Fully describe *what* you want, *who* is included, and *where* it will take place. List your responses in *present* tense. For example, "My wife and I see a Broadway play in New York City" or "I own a successful software company at the Monadnock Building in Chicago."

Do not worry about whether you can afford it; do not dwell on whether it is practical or not. Use this time to list your lifetime goals – we will discuss what to do with your goals later. These statements do not have to be written in one sitting. Enjoy the process.

My Lifetime Goals

It feels great today to start, finish & complete a task, without procrastination

① My present business model of buying/sourcing desirable designer vintage clothes + reselling to wholesale/then to a worldwide I am enjoying the "hunt" & thrill, vintage seeing what treasures are in this estate here in the North West, Southeast, Midwest, Southwest — on the Westcoast I am excited as I get ready the designer vintage

② clothes I am going through now are wonderful, desirable & fun!

I am enjoying the easy relaxed pace of my present carefree existence here in mexico as relaxed today.

From Basic Statements to Concrete Goals

This part of the *Dreams to Action Trailblazer's Guide* is where dreaming meets planning. This is also the stage where many people start to question whether or not they have enough time, resources, or support to persevere with action. You *can* experience your dream – even while you are attending school, employed at a full-time job, taxiing children to activities and athletic events, and juggling multiple responsibilities.

It is impossible to create or pursue what you want unless you *know* what you want. "You were born to win, but to be the winner you were born to be, you have to plan to win and prepare to win," attested Zig Ziglar, author of *Born to Win*. "Then, and only then, can you legitimately *expect* to win."

Brian Tracy insists that those who achieve their dreams "are absolutely clear about their goals and objectives." He explains that only three percent of the adult population has clear, written goals. Tracy adds, "These people accomplish five to ten times as much as people of equal or better education and ability but who, for whatever reason, have never taken the time to write out exactly what they want."

In this section, you will (1) identify an important goal that aligns with your vision and mission and (2) choose tasks that align with your goal. By knowing what you want to achieve, you can plan when, where, and how you must concentrate your efforts.

If you feel frustrated or anxious as you think about defining your goals, you may, as Amy Lynn Andrews, author of *Tell Your Time*, observed, feel "stuck" in one of the following areas:

- You do not know how to define your goals.
- You do not have a plan to pursue your goals.
- You have goals, but do not believe you have the resources to reach your goals.
- You have goals, but do not believe you have the time to reach your goals.
- You have goals, but do not believe you have support from families and friends.

Amy adds, "Recognizing your sticking place will make it a lot easier to overcome."

Creating a plan with manageable goals is an effective way to move from "stuck" to "unstuck." Stephen Covey believed the act of writing goals sets things into motion. "Your mind accepts the challenge and will consciously and unconsciously work to achieve the goal," he said.

SMART Goals

George Doran first used the term, SMART goal, in a 1981 issue of *Management Review*. He explained that a SMART goal is *specific, measurable, attainable, realistic,* and *time-bound*. The act of writing your goals packs your dream with power and sets the dream-to-action process onto a course headed towards success.

I wanted to launch a strong presence on the Internet as a professional speaker and writer. I created the following SMART goal: "I will successfully design a vibrant website that includes a blog and contact information by January 1st."

I scoured the Internet to find quality on-line blogs. I checked out library books about websites. I joined networking groups and talked to people who built their own websites. I watched countless website construction webinars and do-it-yourself website design videos.

I selected Bluehost.com as my web hosting site because I believed they offered outstanding technical support at a very affordable price. I could call and talk to someone who provided technical assistance, ask questions via live chat, obtain valuable information in user forums, and receive website guidance from easy-to-understand video tutorials at the Bluehost Web Hosting Help Center. Within one month, I designed my own WordPress website at DrJulieConnor.com.

The website SMART goal looked like this:

- **SPECIFIC:** I successfully design a vibrant website that includes a blog and contact information by January 1st.

- **MEASURABLE:** My website has two primary components: (1) a blog and (2) contact information.

- **ACHIEVABLE:** I use information from instructional resources, on-line webinars, videos, and tools to steer me throughout the website design process. I contact website designers who offer expert advice. I find exceptional technical support and tutorial guidance at the Bluehost Web Hosting Help Center.

- **REALISTIC:** I possess the creative and innovative knowledge, skills, and resources to design my own website.

- **TIME-BOUND:** I design a website by January 1st.

Defining a SMART goal did not prevent complications. I began my website design journey without a website design vocabulary; I had no words to articulate my questions. However, having a clear and concise SMART goal provided me with direction and a destination. My website design vocabulary and skills improved as I learned new information and applied what I learned to the construction of my website.

think
smart

1 SPECIFIC
2 MEASURABLE
3 ACHIEVABLE
4 REALISTIC
5 TIME-BOUND

How to Craft a SMART Goal

Begin the SMART goal process by rereading your lifetime statements. Select a statement that excites you and fills you with the most passion. This process will allow you to convert your desire into a meaningful, specific goal.

_____

_____

_____

_____

_____

_____

Consider the following questions as you construct a SMART goal:

A SMART goal is **SPECIFIC.**

What do I want to accomplish? _____

_____

_____

_____

_____

_____

Why do I want to accomplish it? _____

_____

_____

_____

_____

_____

What are the benefits? _____

_____

_____

_____

_____

_____

Who is involved? _____

_____

_____

_____

_____

_____

_____

Where will it be accomplished? _____

_____

_____

_____

_____

think
smart

A SMART goal is **MEASURABLE**.

How much is needed? _____
_____
_____
_____
_____
_____

What tools do I need to measure progress? _____
_____
_____
_____
_____
_____

What targets will I establish as I progress towards
my goal? _____
_____
_____
_____
_____
_____

How will I know when it is accomplished?
_____
_____
_____
_____
_____
_____
_____

A SMART goal is **ATTAINABLE**.

How can my goal be accomplished? _____
_____
_____
_____
_____
_____

How is my goal action-oriented? _____
_____
_____
_____
_____
_____

How much will it cost to launch and support
my goal? _____
_____
_____
_____
_____
_____

What knowledge and skills are needed to reach this goal?
_____
_____
_____
_____
_____
_____

A SMART goal is **REALISTIC.**

Why is my goal meaningful? _____

_____

_____

_____

_____

_____

Why is there a need for this goal? _____

_____

_____

_____

_____

_____

Why is this the right time to pursue this goal?

_____

_____

_____

_____

_____

Is this goal aligned with my core values?

_____

_____

_____

_____

_____

A SMART goal is **TIME-BOUND.**

What is the time frame for implementation of this goal? _____

_____

_____

_____

When will this plan be implemented? _____

_____

_____

_____

What will I do *within the next six months* to reach my goal? _____

_____

_____

_____

What will I do *within the next six weeks* to reach my goal? _____

_____

_____

_____

_____

What will I do *this week* to reach my goal?

_____

_____

_____

Powerful Tips for Writing SMART Goals

Here are additional tips to consider as you compose your SMART goals:

- **State each goal as a positive statement.** Express your goals with positive words.

  Rather than stating *"Don't be afraid to contact clients,"* say *"I confidently contact ten clients this week."*

- **Be precise.** Set specific goals; include dates, times, and measurable amounts so you can track your progress.

  Rather than stating *"Use social media to build a following as a health coach,"* say *"I post quality content across social media platforms at 7am, noon, and 4pm every day to promote health and wellness."*

- **Set objective performance goals.** As you write goals, use action verbs that can be observed and measured as opposed to abstract and subjective goals.

  Rather than stating *"Become a more collaborative staff,"* say *"I invite our staff to participate in brainstorming sessions every Wednesday morning at 10am."*

- **Set priorities.** Prioritizing tasks protects you from feeling overwhelmed and anxious by focusing your attention on important choices and activities that are directly connected to your goals. Clarify your priorities so you can make the best use of your time.

"Do a careful analysis of your starting point before you set off toward the achievement of your goal," suggests Brian Tracy in his book, *Goals!: How to Get Everything You Want.* "Determine your exact situation today and be both honest and realistic about what you want to accomplish in the future."

- **Arrange time in your schedule to pursue your passions.** Finding creative ways to fit specific tasks aligned with your goals into your schedule takes work and effort. You must consider how much time you have within a twenty-four hour period that can be devoted to tasks that will help you meet your goals.

There are more helpful time management tips in the chapter, *Plan It! Maximize Your Time.* We will explore specific means through which you can build time into your schedule to accomplish your goals.

Use the information from your responses to compose a SMART goal statement that is *specific, measurable, attainable, realistic,* and *time-bound.*

My SMART GOAL

_____

_____

_____

_____

_____

_____

_____

_____

_____

Richard G. Scott said, "We become what we want to be by consistently being what we want to become each day." Commitment is crucial to the development of a successful action plan.

As you write your goals and, more importantly, review and revise them, you will make conscious choices that lead you to greater success. You will experience greater confidence as you watch your desired goals unfold in your life.

- **Writing goals provides you with clarity.** The more specifically you define your goals, the more vibrantly you can visualize them and set a course of action into motion.

- **Writing goals provides a filter for other opportunities.** There are many activities, responsibilities, and distractions that compete for your attention. Goal alignment allows you to make meaningful choices.

- **Writing goals helps you to overcome resistance.** Every meaningful intention or desire encounters struggle or opposition. Focus on your goal, not on the things that block you from achieving your goal.

- **Writing goals enable you to see and celebrate progress.** Like mile markers on a highway, goals enable you to see how far you have come. They provide opportunities for celebration when you attain them.

The more specifically you define your goals, the more enthusiastic you become about your dream. Napoleon Hill, author of *Think and Grow Rich,* said, "What the mind of man can conceive, it can achieve." Make a commitment to yourself and to your dream. We will discuss how to take the necessary steps to reach your goals in the next chapter, *Plan It! Sculpt Your Goals Into Priorities.*

Write Your GOALS

PLAN IT! DEFINE YOUR GOALS

A clear sense of purpose aligned with your goals and core values directs your attention to extraordinary opportunities. Focused intent on *what* you want and *why* you want it helps you shed limiting self-doubts and draws you into your creative power of confidence and positive expectation.

"In preparation for planning your path, understand that you don't have to know precisely how to reach your goals and live your intention when you set out on your journey," explains Dr. Michelle Robin, author of *The E Factor: Engage, Energize, Enrich.* "All you need to know is the next best step." She encourages us to allow our intention to serve as our directional compass.

Your Annual Goals

In this section, you can craft your "bucket list" or lifetime goals into smaller, more manageable chunks that can be shaped into meaningful and important targets. Create concrete, specific goals in each of the following areas: *spiritual goals, health and wellness goals, social and emotional goals, family goals, mental* and *intellectual goals, career and educational goals,* and *financial goals.* Allow the questions in each section to guide your responses.

Spiritual Goals

Do I have a regular practice of prayer or meditation? Do I read and listen to material that feeds my spiritual growth? What activities cultivate my spirituality? Do I belong to a spiritual community? How would I like to become more actively involved in spiritual community activities?

_____

_____

Health & Wellness Goals

How much do I want to weigh? What changes in my diet would I like to make? Do I exercise? Do I get enough sleep? How do I take care of my body? What lifestyle changes can I make to improve my health?

_____

_____

_____

_____

_____

_____

_____

_____

_____

_____

_____

_____

_____

Social & Emotional Goals

Do I feel confident? Does fear prevent me from pursuing my passions? Do I feel unconditionally loved by someone? Do I have one or more close friends? Do I have a support system? Do I have hobbies? Do I take part in social activities? How am I involved in active service to others?

_____
_____
_____
_____
_____
_____
_____
_____
_____
_____

Family Goals

How do I define my family? What family activities are important to me? How do we celebrate holidays and important events? How do we communicate and resolve conflict? What can I do to more effectively support my family members? What do I need to feel supported by my family?

_____
_____
_____
_____

_____
_____
_____
_____
_____
_____
_____
_____

Mental & Intellectual Goals

What new skills or information would I like to learn? Where would I like to learn it? What training is available? What sources of information are available? How can I include learning opportunities in my schedule?

_____
_____
_____
_____
_____
_____
_____
_____
_____
_____

Career & Educational Goals

What is my ideal job? Where do I want to work? What skills and knowledge do I use or need to maintain or pursue my career and educational goals? How can I learn new skills and knowledge? Where can I learn new skills and knowledge? What financial or educational resources are available?

_____
_____
_____
_____
_____
_____
_____
_____
_____
_____
_____
_____
_____

Financial Goals

How much money would I like to earn? What resources are available to finance other goals? How much would I like to save? What would I like to purchase? How would I like to invest my wealth? How would I like to invest in my children's futures? How much would I like to set aside for my retirement? How would I like to share my wealth with others?

_____
_____
_____
_____
_____
_____
_____
_____
_____
_____
_____
_____

LIGHT YOUR PASSION

YOUR MONTHLY GOALS

Take another look at your annual goals. Select target goals you would like to pursue throughout the upcoming month. The number of monthly goals you choose will vary depending upon the complexity and amount of time you need to invest in the completion of each one.

Write your goals in complete sentences and in *present* tense. For example, if one of your social and emotional goals is to become more involved in your community, you may consider, "I volunteer to read stories to kindergartners at our local elementary school."

Some people are capable of creating and completing more than twenty monthly goals; I usually compose five to seven monthly goals. You may generate a list of goals related to one specific area (i.e.: career goal). Or you may choose to explore multiple goals. Incorporate elements of SMART goal planning into your statements. A step forward is a step in the right direction.

During the Month of _____, I ...

Your Weekly Goals

Review your selection of monthly goals. Choose one to ten goals you would like to pursue this week. I typically create three to six primary goals every week. Some weekly goals become part of my regular routine. Some of the tasks from previous weeks must be subdivided into different, more specific goals.

As always, be specific and write your goals in *present* tense. Practice visualization; experience the wonderful sensation of accomplishment as if you have already reached your goals.

During the Week of _____, I ...

_____
_____
_____
_____
_____
_____
_____
_____
_____
_____
_____
_____
_____
_____
_____
_____
_____
_____
_____
_____

Your Daily Priorities

Examine the goals you selected for the week. Describe specific tasks that will help you reach your weekly goals. Assign different tasks to the days of the week in the spaces below.

"Your most important tasks and priorities are those that can have the most serious consequences, positive or negative, on your life or work," explains Brian Tracy. "Focus on these above all else." Your goals and the tasks you choose to accomplish your goals either align with dream and core values or they don't. It's that simple.

Monday

_____
_____
_____
_____
_____
_____
_____
_____
_____
_____
_____
_____
_____
_____
_____
_____

Tuesday

_____
_____
_____
_____
_____
_____
_____
_____
_____
_____
_____
_____
_____
_____
_____
_____
_____

Wednesday

_____
_____
_____
_____
_____
_____
_____
_____
_____
_____
_____
_____

Thursday

_____
_____
_____
_____
_____
_____
_____
_____
_____
_____
_____
_____
_____
_____
_____
_____

Friday

_____
_____
_____
_____
_____
_____
_____
_____
_____
_____

Saturday

Sunday

Remember to ask yourself, "Are the responsibilities and tasks I identify as important priorities connected to my vision, mission, and goals?" Activities aligned with what you want to be, do, and experience provide ways for you to more acutely see how every step, every accomplishment, and each daily achievement moves you closer to your dream.

We will explore how to build time into your agenda to reach your goals in the next chapter, *Plan It! Maximize Your Time.* You will discover you have more time to do the things you love to do because you found ways to include the things that give your life the most meaning and joy into your busy day.

PLAN IT! MAXIMIZE YOUR TIME

You resourcefully created a list of your deepest desires and fashioned them into goals in the previous chapter, *Plan It! Sculpt Goals Into Priorities*. In this chapter, you will discover how you can incorporate specific tasks connected to your goals into your schedule.

But how do you break down an enormous goal that has so many tasks? What tasks should you select if you don't know what must be done to reach your goal? How can you add more tasks to a packed calendar if you feel overburdened with too many responsibilities already? It's very much like eating a colossal elephant – you begin by eating it one bite at a time.

No matter how many activities are piled on your calendar, you only have twenty-four hours within each day to complete your most important tasks. Remember you have choices. As you become more aware of your habits and how you choose to make the most of the time you have available, you will choose activities that align with your goals and assert your personal prioritizing power.

Your time is a precious commodity. Sometimes it is difficult to choose between multiple important priorities. "I think you should spend less time doing what you *have* to do and more time doing what you were *made* to do," maintains Amy Lynn Andrews. "But in order for that to happen, you must avoid adding things to your calendar simply because there is space. Be thoughtful. Be deliberate."

Finding time within your schedule for tasks and activities that move you closer to accomplishing your goals is not nearly as difficult as backing out of activities and commitments you regret making in the first place. When you streamline your schedule by making deliberate decisions about tasks and activities that are crucially important to you and identify your most important priorities, you give yourself permission to make choices that excite and interest you. You also grant yourself permission to exercise your right to say, "No, thank you."

Your Planning Table

A tool such as MY PLANNING TABLE helps you balance your most important priorities and find time in your schedule to do what you most want to do. As you plan, it is important to distinguish between the urgency and importance of your daily tasks and responsibilities.

The *urgency* of an activity is connected to time. A last-minute report due at noon today is an urgent issue. The *importance* of an issue is tied to its value or significance. A weekly staff conference, for example, is an important priority. Although some of your daily activities may be both urgent and important, addressing important tasks and activities before they become urgent emergencies is an essential element of time management.

The vertical columns of the planning table contain spaces for *nonnegotiable activities* and *negotiable activities*; they reflect issues of importance. Nonnegotiable activities include commitments that are critical personal obligations. Negotiable activities may be enjoyable and fulfilling, but they are not necessarily essential priorities. You can choose whether you want to participate in negotiable activities – or not.

Attending church services is very important to me; this is a *nonnegotiable* commitment on my planning table. I plan other things around nonnegotiable activities. I enjoy yoga classes and I want to make time to attend them, but I will skip yoga if I have a speaking engagement or family obligation. Yoga class is a *negotiable* or less important activity.

Horizontal rows contain activities that occur at *fixed times* and *flexible* (or *flex) times*. Activities that take place at fixed times are determined by someone else; you have the freedom to choose what time you want to participate in flex time activities. The urgency of an activity is dependent upon how quickly it must be addressed.

For example, I teach a college course at a *fixed time* determined by the university. This is a nonnegotiable responsibility and an important priority.

I post an article on my blog at DrJulieConnor. com every Monday morning at a time determined by me (or *flex time*). This is a nonnegotiable and urgent task on Monday mornings, but other responsibilities take precedence over blog writing later in the week. I build time in my schedule to begin writing it on Thursdays so I do not feel frantic on Mondays. On Thursdays, writing my blog post is less urgent, but it is still an important activity.

Negotiable activities are typically enjoyable but less urgent than nonnegotiable activities because they are not critical priorities. Unlike nonnegotiable activities; I choose whether or not I want to participate in negotiable activities. I enjoy being a member of my book club, but I do not attend book club gatherings if an urgent responsibility arises on Wednesday evenings because it occurs at a *fixed time*. I periodically meet friends for lunch because this is a *flex time* activity; my friends and I get together at a time that best fits our schedules.

As you think about activities and responsibilities to insert in MY PLANNING TABLE, consider whether your tasks are nonnegotiable or negotiable activities occurring at fixed or flexible times:

- **Nonnegotiable Activities at Fixed Times (P1):** Important priorities and obligations that occur at times determined by someone else.
- **Nonnegotiable Activities at Flex Times (P2):** Important priorities and obligations that occur at a time set by you.
- **Negotiable Activities at Fixed Times (P3):** Activities you may want to participate in at times determined by someone else.
- **Negotiable Activities at Flex Times (P4):** Activities you may want to take participate in at a time set by you.

The planning table will allow you to identify and distinguish between your most important priorities. This information will help you clarify your priorities and determine where and how you want to allocate your time. I included examples of activities on my planning table. You can find a full-page copy of MY PLANNING TABLE for your use in the appendix.

MY PLANNING TABLE

NONNEGOTIABLE ACTIVITIES	NEGOTIABLE ACTIVITIES
Tasks & Responsibilities I Must Do Time Pre-Determined (P1)	**Tasks & Responsibilities I Can Do Time Pre-Determined (P3)**
Teach College Course Weekly Team Planning Meeting Attend Church Services	Yoga Class Book Club ARTS Group
Tasks & Responsibilities I Must Do Time Determined by Me (P2)	**Tasks & Responsibilities I Can Do Time Determined by Me (P4)**
Speaking & Workshop Engagements Blog Post Social Networking	Movie/Date Night Lunch with Friends Edit Research

FIXED TIME (applies to P1 and P3 rows)
FLEX TIME (applies to P2 and P4 rows)

Your Weekly Schedule

Time management is crucial if you want to achieve your goals. Once you identify activities that are important to you, you can determine how much time is needed to complete certain tasks. MY WEEKLY SCHEDULE is a chart that will help you organize your time and tasks.

Refer to MY PLANNING TABLE as you add nonnegotiable and negotiable tasks to your schedule. Include your most important *nonnegotiable* tasks and commitments that are held at *fixed times* (refer to Quadrant P1) to your schedule before you add anything else. Decide which days and at what time you would like to schedule *nonnegotiable/flex time* activities (Quadrant P2).

Add *negotiable* activities from Quadrants P3 and P4 after you have allocated adequate time for your most important priorities. I build cushions of time in my schedule for interruptions or urgent matters that may arise throughout the day. You will have time to address issues that arise unexpectedly if you plan well, work smart, and tackle your most important tasks first.

Remember to allow time for sleep, meals, and adequate transportation time to and from events. When you understand how to plan and use your time, you can adapt and make changes to your schedule. You can reduce the amount of time you spend doing some activities to devote more time to goal-related tasks. You may choose to delete some tasks entirely from your schedule.

I included a summary of tasks and events on my weekly schedule. A copy of **MY WEEKLY SCHEDULE** for your use is available in the appendix of this book.

MY WEEKLY SCHEDULE

	SUN.	MON.	TUES.	WED.	THUR.	FRI.	SAT.
6:00 am - 6:30 am	Prayer/Goals	Prayer/Goals	Prayer/Goals	Prayer/Goals	Prayer/Goals	Prayer/Goals	Prayer/Goals
6:30 am - 7:00 am	Breakfast	Breakfast	Breakfast	Breakfast	Breakfast	Breakfast	Breakfast
7:00 am - 8:00 am	Family Time	Post Blog	Newsletter	Networking	Write Blog	Write Blog	Family Time
8:00 am - 8:30 am		Soc. Media	Soc. Media	Soc. Media	Soc. Media	Soc. Media	
8:30 am - 9:00 am		Mail/eMail	Mail/eMail	Mail/eMail	Mail/eMail	Mail/eMail	
9:00 am - 9:30 am							Family Time
9:30 am - 10:00 am		Phone Calls	Phone Calls	Phone Calls	Phone Calls	Phone Calls	Household Chores
10:00 am - 11:00 am	Church	College Course Prep	Event Preparation	College Course Prep	Event Preparation	Host Webinar	
11:00 am - 11:30 am	Lunch	Lunch	Lunch	Lunch	Lunch	Lunch	Lunch
11:30 am - 12:00 pm							
12:00 pm - 1:00 pm	MasterMind	College Course	Workshop	College Course	Workshop	Conference	ARTS Group
1:00 pm - 2:00 pm							
2:00 pm - 2:30 pm	Family Time						Grocery Shopping
2:30 pm - 3:00 pm		Workshop Prep	Workshop Prep	Workshop Prep	Workshop Prep	Workshop Prep	
3:00 pm - 3:30 pm		Read & Research	Book Engagements	Read & Research	Book Engagements	Week Assessment	Yoga Class
3:30 pm - 4:00 pm							
4:00 pm - 5:00 pm		Calls/eMail	Calls/eMail	Calls/eMail	Calls/eMail	Calls/eMail	
5:00 pm - 5:30 pm	Walk Dog	Walk Dog	Walk Dog	Walk Dog	Walk Dog	Walk Dog	Walk Dog
5:30 am - 6:30 pm	Family Time	Dinner	Dinner	Dinner	Dinner	Dinner	Date Night
6:30 pm - 7:00 pm							
7:00 pm - 7:30 pm	Calls/eMail	Workshop	Family Time	Book Club	Workshop	Date Night	
7:30 pm - 8:00 pm	Weekly Calendar						
8:00 pm - 8:30 pm							
8:30 pm - 9:00 pm	Finish Blog			Family Time			
9:00 pm - 9:30 pm							
09:30 pm -10:00 pm	Read	Read	Read	Read	Read	Read	Read
10:00 pm - 6:00 am	Sleep	Sleep	Sleep	Sleep	Sleep	Sleep	Sleep

Arrange time to regularly review your calendar and goals each week. I thoroughly assess my achievements and challenges on Friday afternoons. I examine activities and weekly tasks listed on my calendar on Monday mornings. This provides me with an opportunity to ensure my goals and tasks are aligned with my vision and mission statements.

Napoleon Hill believed, "Procrastination is the bad habit of putting off until the day after tomorrow what should have been done the day before yesterday." Deliberate planning permits you to make the best use of your time and moves you more quickly towards your dream.

Make Time Work for You

As you make decisions about how you want to use your time each day, you must remember that the *total number of hours* available to you is *less than 24 hours*. If you find you have too many activities crammed into a 24-hour period, make adjustments. To allow time in your schedule for activities that give your life purpose and meaning, you may need to (1) reduce the amount of time spent on less important tasks or less enjoyable commitments, (2) increase the amount of time you would like to devote to goal-related activities, (3) find someone to help you complete some of your tasks, or (4) remove less important tasks or less enjoyable commitments from your schedule.

Your weekly calendar is a fluid work in progress. It is not carved in stone. You may want to remove some tasks to make room for extracurricular activities, family events, and important engagements. Adding a block of time to your schedule each week to make mindful decisions about what you want to do and when you want to do it puts you in charge of your calendar.

Commit to making the most efficient use of time as you transition between events throughout the day. For example, I tend to be a perfectionist and I want everything I do to be done well. I could spend exorbitant amounts of time re-correcting written work if I did not set time limits (such as time I allow to write my weekly blog at DrJulieConnor.com). When I mismanage time in one area, it affects all of the other tasks on my schedule.

If we give ourselves permission to waste time or obsess about details of certain tasks, we spend the rest of the day "stealing" time from other activities that need our attention. I use a timer throughout the day as I move between tasks. A timer and use of the Pomodoro Technique help me focus and make quality use of my time.

Francesco Cirillo developed the Pomodoro Technique as a system of time management. He used a tomato-shaped timer and subdivided work into 25 minute intervals that were separated by short breaks. He called the breaks "pomodori" (from the Italian word, "pomodoro," or "tomato"). He based his method on the belief that frequent breaks throughout the day improved mental agility. I find that a timer is an invaluable tool that allows me to stay focused on tasks and manage my time well.

Time management "is really *life* management," explains Brian Tracy. Practical management of your time includes taking responsibility of your choices. Tracy insists that your ability to discern important from trivial tasks "is the key determinant of your success in life and work."

The 80/20 Principle

In 1906, Italian economist Vilfredo Pareto created a mathematical formula that reflected unequal distribution of wealth; he concluded that 80% of the land and its assets were controlled by 20% of its people. Joseph Juran expanded Pareto's socioeconomic observations to include a broader, more universal application of what he called the 80/20 relationship of the "vital few and the trivial many." He suggested the Pareto Principle to industries as a means to improve systemic flaws and make meaningful improvements.

Richard Koch, author of *The 80/20 Principle: The Secret of Achieving More with Less,* provided practical applications of this principle to time management strategies. He explained that about 20% of what we do produces 80% of our desired outcomes. He stated that a typical 80/20 pattern shows that "80% of consequences flow from 20% of causes; or that 80% of results comes from 20% of effort." He adds that we spend about 20% of our time engaged in activities that produce about 80% of our greatest happiness and give our lives the most meaning.

When the Pareto Principal is applied to your time management choices, you recognize that 80% of your most productive work generally comes from about 20% of your time committed to your work. About 20% of the things listed on most people's calendars are activities that produce the greatest and most satisfying results.

What are the things that, when done well, reflect the highest quality of your work? What tasks produce your most valuable results? If you are completing your core tasks with excellence in mind, you devote your best efforts to your most important responsibilities.

Maximizing your use of time is a critical time management skill. Recognizing and focusing on your most important tasks and priorities is key to making the most effective use of your time. Take a look at your schedule and examine how you choose to spend your time. Ask yourself:

- Are the tasks and activities on my schedule aligned with my goals?

- What tasks contribute most significantly to my success?

- What are my most important responsibilities?

- In what areas am I wasting time?

- What areas need more of my attention?

What are your most important daily priorities? For example, you may need a strong social media presence to launch your dream. However, if you devote eight hours each day to work and spend four hours reading posts and engaging in on-line social media conversations, that means 50% of your work time is spent on the Internet. Do you draw customer traffic from social media interactions? Are you consciously using your time in ways that allow you to pursue your passions? When you become clear about *what* you do and *how long* you choose to do it, you reconsider how your choices best serve your personal and professional interests.

Value Your Time

It is crucial to keep your dream and your vision and mission statements in mind as you select activities for your calendar. As you plan your schedule, think about the following questions:

- Do my daily activities represent things *I want to do* or are they activities I believe I am *required to* do?

- Am I obligated to participate in activities out of guilt or fear of what others will think?

- Do I allow others to dictate how I should plan my time and choose priorities?

- Do activities and tasks on my calendar align with my goals and core values?

- Do activities and tasks on my calendar align with my vision and mission statements?

- Do the activities and tasks on my calendar move me closer to my dream?

Some activities and tasks cannot be easily dropped. For example, it may be impossible to enroll in art classes at night if you coach a winter league basketball team. That should not stop you from making a commitment to draw on a regular basis. Nor should it prevent you from exploring weekend or spring semester classes.

Although you may work at two jobs, there are many on-line educational opportunities and webinars that offer the skills and knowledge to accomplish your goals at times you have available. You may be a stay-at-home mother who committed to carpooling neighborhood children to and from school. There is nothing "wrong" about reworking the carpool agreement with the children's parents if you want time to write your book. That qualifies as a new job.

Your dream, vision statement, mission statement, and goals anchor you in the direction you want to pursue. The most important questions to consider as you make choices include:

- How do I want to make a *difference* in the world?

- How do I want to be *remembered*?

- What kind of *legacy* do I want to leave behind?

Be deliberate in your choices. We are created to do what we believe we are called to do and what we are born to experience, not what we believe other people expect us to do. Your time is precious.

Handy Calendar Tips

There are many different types of planners and calendars that will help you organize your activities and tasks. I depend upon Google Calendar; it links my on-line calendar to my cell phone. I can print copies to keep in a pocket in my briefcase or share it with others. I color-code events on my calendar because I find it visually easier to distinguish between tasks.

Some people rely on FranklinCovey planning products and their impressive on-line tools. Others happily use free calendars from grocery stores and local churches. The *type* of planning tool you select is not nearly as important as the *consistency* with which you use the tools.

Listed below are tips you may find helpful as you organize your calendar:

- **Color-code calendar events** with different colored pens or highlighters to keep track of regularly scheduled events.

- Select a **calendar that includes holidays** and important reoccurring events.

- Place **Post-It Notes by your family calendar** for family members to add personal events. (This is particularly helpful if one person is responsible for managing the calendar.)

- **Mark or set alerts on your calendar to remind you of upcoming events.** Include alerts of special events if you send cards or presents to special loved ones.

- **Set deadlines and project completion dates** on your calendar. Deadlines will help you plan for and commit to efficient use of your time.

- Mark or set on-line alerts within your schedule to remind you to **change tasks and begin projects** throughout your work day.

Tips to organize your calendar!

DO IT! KICK IT INTO GEAR

Once you begin your dream adventure, you must find resources and develop habits to stay motivated and enthused as you continue your journey. Persistent effort invested in the following practices will keep you inspired and motivated.

Discover Motivational Resources

Find inspiration by posting quotations from your favorite trailblazers and role models in your home and work space. Read magazine and journal articles, books, and audio resources by trailblazers who stand where you want to go. Explore Internet resources, go to the library, check out on-line groups, and talk to like-minded individuals who are eager to recommend resources that will keep you inspired. There is an enormous amount of information composed by experts in your chosen field who willingly share their progress, setbacks, and achievements that they experienced on their roads to success.

Universities and libraries offer free and minimal cost workshops and courses that are taught by quality instructors. Many school districts and community centers host programs that provide information and skill training that may be helpful to you as you pursue your goals. There are also excellent on-line webinars, courses, and audio-visual resources that provide exceptional learning opportunities.

The Internet is packed with free "how-to" video resources across a wide spectrum of areas and interests that teach and provide supportive coaching as you master new skills. Technology offers incredible tools which empower us to change the world.

Compose Positive Affirmations

The most effective way to transform the quality of your life is to transform your perception of yourself. Positive affirmations quiet negative thoughts and strengthen your ability to focus deliberate intention on a desired outcome. When you declare a positive affirmation, you acknowledge your own strengths and gifts and confidently invite positive results into your reality.

Positive affirmations are always stated in present tense. They are personal and specific. A statement such as "I let go of all of my previous failures and try not to be discouraged" invites regret and mentally prepares you for more experiences of failure and discouragement. A constructive affirmation such as "I embrace all learning opportunities that contribute to my success and celebrate my achievements" reflects gratitude for previous experiences, openness to new ideas, and acknowledges your accomplishments. This shift in perspective welcomes wonderful opportunities and greater success.

Positive affirmations are effective because neurons in your brain interpret imagery as reality equivalents. When you visualize something and state your intention in positive terms with positive outcomes, the brain generates impulses that create new neural pathways that prepare you to perform in ways that are consistent to what you imagined. As you write and access the creative energy of the right brain, you open your mind to solutions you may have not ordinarily considered.

"Your life doesn't just 'happen.' Whether you know it or not, it is carefully designed by you," insisted Stephen Covey. "The choices, after all, are yours. You choose happiness. You choose sadness. You choose decisiveness. You choose ambivalence. You choose success. You choose failure." He added, "Just remember that every moment, every situation, provides a new choice. And in doing so, it gives you a perfect opportunity to do things differently to produce more positive results."

There is no such thing as "empty words." Every thought you have and every word you speak influences your choices, decisions, and actions. You either move towards your goals or push them away. Positive affirmations (including these potent examples) provide you with opportunities to purge anger, relinquish fear, create your own future, and joyfully experience the enormous potential within you:

- I am the architect of my life; I use my gifts and talents to build a strong foundation.
- I am filled with energy and overflowing with joy.
- My relationships with family members are strong, loving, and stable.
- My business is growing, expanding, and thriving.
- Lucrative opportunities bless my life with abundance and prosperity.
- Creative energy fills me with new and brilliant ideas.
- I face today with strength of heart and clarity of mind.
- My heart is tranquil and I am at peace.
- I am courageous and bold. I have within me the power to change the world.

Use Vibrant Visualizations

Visualization allows you to imagine a desired outcome and what you want to see manifested in your life. This practice allows you to "see" yourself experiencing success through the power of imagination. Visualization is a "mental rehearsal" of success; it is a technique of performance improvement consistently supported by scientific evidence and used by many successful individuals across professions. Athletic champions experience success many, many times before record-breaking events by visualizing themselves executing brilliant performances and standing on gold medal platforms long before they were recognized for their achievements.

At one of the lowest points in my life, I was plagued with panic attacks. My father died from a heart attack and I was afraid each bout of anxiety would be fatal. Panic attacks exploded into full-blown agoraphobia. I was afraid to leave my home. A friend found an old audio cassette tape at a hospital. The audio cassette contained guided meditations that allowed me to use visualizations to relax my mind and body. Repeated practice of visualizations released me from the bondage of panic and allowed me to reengage with others and find new freedom to pursue my dreams.

As you use visualizations to pursue your goals, imagine specific details about your involvement in success-filled achievements. See and experience events and outcomes and as if you already reached your goal. Consider these questions as you envision experiences of personal accomplishments:

- What are you doing when you reach your goal?
- How do you feel when you are engaged in tasks that promote your success?
- Where are you working?
- Who works with you?
- Who are you serving?
- How do you celebrate your success?
- Who celebrates with you?

Visualization prepares you for the experience of success. As you become increasingly optimistic, excited, and motivated about ideas that motivate you, you open yourself to new ideas, meaningful relationships, and exhilarating opportunities.

Connect with a Support System

Surround yourself with people who eagerly encourage you and celebrate your success. Build supportive relationships:

- **Find a mentor or accountability partner.** Reach out to someone who has a similar goal. Share your progress at regularly scheduled times to discuss goals, celebrate accomplishments, and hold each other accountable for completing goal-related tasks.

- **Join a mastermind group.** The term "mastermind group" was first coined by Napoleon Hill in his book, *Think and Grow Rich*. Participants in a mastermind group brainstorm and support one another. Similar to accountability partners, mastermind group members collaboratively share new ideas, offer fresh solutions, provide honest feedback, and encourage one another as they pursue their goals.

- **Network with others.** Find a group with members who share your professional or goal-related interests. Many groups and organizations have well-organized and detailed directories that promote networking events and attract new members. Local Chamber of Commerce groups, libraries, and community centers provide information and resources within your community.

- **Discover on-line networking groups.** Most reputable networking groups have strong on-line platforms. Many social media groups provide opportunities for individuals to build a professional on-line presence and network with other like-minded individuals with shared hobbies, interests, and professions. A growing number of networks allow groups and communities to take part in video meetings. There are also cloud platforms that allow you to share files with others and manage projects as a collaborative group.

Dr. Gail Matthews, psychology professor at Dominican University of California, conducted a study to learn how commitment affected successful goal achievement. She found that individuals who (1) expressed their goals in *writing*, (2) developed action statements, and (3) held themselves accountable to a friend, colleague, or mentor were 76% more likely to experience success than those whose goals were cloaked in daydreams.

Stephen Covey agreed there was meaningful value in sharing your goals with another person. "The momentum picks up if you tell someone your goal," he added. "The act of stating your goal creates a sense of accountability for its completion."

Celebrate Success

It is important to reward yourself and recognize your achievements. Past success reflects your progress; future celebrations give us something to look forward to. Celebrations of weekly, monthly, and annual goals build self-confidence and fill you with the enthusiasm and stamina needed to reach future goals.

Celebrations do not have to be elaborate or expensive. It does not matter whether you celebrate your achievements by yourself (with a pedicure or purchase of a new novel) or with others by inviting them to a special event or meal. Celebrate your successes soon after you reach a goal.

Marianne Williamson, author of *A Return to Love: Reflections on the Principles of A Course in Miracles*, eloquently writes:

> Our deepest fear is not that we are inadequate. Our deepest fear is that we are powerful beyond measure. It is our light, not our darkness that most frightens us. We ask ourselves, "Who am I to be brilliant, gorgeous, talented, fabulous?" Actually, who are you *not* to be? You are a child of God. Your playing small does not serve the world. There is nothing enlightened about shrinking so that other people won't feel insecure around you. We are all meant to shine, as children do. We were born to make manifest the glory of God that is within us. It's not just in some of us; it's in everyone. And as we let our own light shine, we unconsciously give other people permission to do the same. As we are liberated from our own fear, our presence automatically liberates others.

Share your good news with others. Announcements of your achievements encourage others to pursue their passions. Celebrations and rewards remind us how far we have come and why we invested so much of ourselves into a passionate pursuit of a dream in the first place.

CONCLUSION

The purpose of the *Dreams to Action Trailblazer's Guide* was to provide you with a framework to define your dream, develop meaningful vision and mission statements, create tangible goals, and design a practical structure that allows you to transform your dream into manageable chunks that can be incorporated into your daily routine. Your responses to exercises in this workbook invited you to:

- **Dream It** – You described your dream and goals that aligned with your vision and mission statements.

- **Plan It** – You outlined tasks and responsibilities. You arranged time within your calendar to engage in meaningful goal-related activities.

Now, you must:

- **Do It** – Take action and commit to doing the work you outlined to reach your goals.

Continue to network with those who support you and your vision. Be open to learning new information. Look for resources that will help you refine your skills. You can find many resources that will help you pursue your passions with confidence on my website at DrJulieConnor.com.

Passion fuels dreams. Commitment fuels action. Get clear about what you want to do and why you want to do it. Allow time to regularly reevaluate and refine your goals. Make adjustments within your schedule to engage in goal-related activities. And, most importantly, commit to the work of pursuing your dream. Take action.

Your time is now!

APPENDIX

Use the following worksheets to articulate your gifts and talents, identify skills and information you would like to attain, distinguish your priorities, and successfully plot activities and tasks on a timetable that will lead you to your dream.

- **My Skills and Knowledge Chart**
- **My Planning Table**
- **My Weekly Schedule**

MY SKILLS AND KNOWLEDGE CHART

Use this chart to (1) acknowledge the knowledge and talents you presently possess and (2) list skills and information that will help you successfully complete tasks, step into future roles, and reach your goals in the future.

SKILLS I Have	SKILLS I Want
KNOWLEDGE I Have	KNOWLEDGE I Want

MY PLANNING TABLE

As you think about activities and responsibilities to include in this table, consider whether each task is a *negotiable* or *nonnegotiable* activity occurring at a *fixed* or *flexible time*. The information you include in this chart will help you distinguish between your most important responsibilities, clarify priorities, and determine how and when you want to allocate your time.

	NONNEGOTIABLE ACTIVITIES	NEGOTIABLE ACTIVITIES
Fixed Time	*Tasks & Responsibilities I Must Do Time Pre-Determined (P1)*	*Tasks & Responsibilities I Can Do Time Pre-Determined (P3)*
Flex Time	*Tasks & Responsibilities I Must Do Time Determined by Me (P2)*	*Tasks & Responsibilities I Can Do Time Determined by Me (P4)*

MY WEEKLY SCHEDULE

This schedule will help you organize your time and tasks. Begin by writing your most important *nonnegotiable* activities from **MY PLANNING TABLE** on this chart. Add *negotiable* activities after you allocated adequate time for your most important priorities

TIME	Sun.	Mon.	Tues.	Wed.	Thurs.	Fri.	Sat.

BIBLIOGRAPHY

Andrews, A. (2011). *Tell Your Time: How to Manage Your Schedule So You Can Live Free* (Kindle Locations 568-569). Amy Lynn Andrews. Kindle Edition.

Bratskeir, K. (2013, April 25). Positive Affirmations: 10 De-Stressing Phrases That Help Put Life Into Perspective. *The Huffington Post*. Retrieved from http://www.huffingtonpost.com/2013/04/25/positive-affirmations-de-stressing-mantras_n_3047604.html

Brown, B. (2012). *Daring Greatly*. New York, NY: Gotham.

Coelho, P. (1994). *The Alchemist*. (A. Clarke, Trans.). New York, NY: HarperCollins. (Original work published 1988).

Covey, S. (2004). *The 7 Habits of Highly Effective People: Powerful Lessons in Personal Change* (2nd ed.). New York, NY: Simon & Schuster.

Dooley, M. (2011). *Leveraging the Universe: 7 Steps to Engaging the Magic*. New York, NY: Simon & Schuster.

Doran, G. (1981). There's a S.M.A.R.T. Way to Write Management's Goals and Objectives. *Management Review* (AMA Forum), 70(2), 35-36.

Gerber, M. (2008). *Awakening the Entrepreneur Within: How Ordinary People Can Create Extraordinary Companies*. New York, NY: Collins.

Hill, N. (2012). *Think and Grow Rich!: The Original 1937 Unedited Edition*. [Kindle DX version]. Retrieved from Amazon.com

Iacocca, L. (1984). *Iacocca: An Autobiography*. W. Novak, ed. New York, NY: Bantam.

Koch, R. (2008). *The 80/20 Principle: The Secret of Achieving More with Less* (2nd ed.). New York, NY: Doubleday.

Kouzes, J., & Posner, B. (2012). *The Leadership Challenge* (4th ed.). San Francisco, CA: Jossey-Bass.

Matthews, G. (n.d.). *Goals Research Summary*. Retrieved from http://www.dominican.edu/academics/ahss/undergraduate-programs-1/psych/faculty/full-time/gailmatthews/researchsummary2.pdf

Maxwell, J. (2008). *Put Your Dream to the Test: 10 Questions That Will Help You See It and Seize It*. Nashville, TN: Thomas Nelson.

Morrissey, M. (1997). *Building Your Field of Dreams*. New York, NY: Bantham.

Robin, M. (2012). *The E Factor: Engage, Energize, Enrich: Three Steps to Vibrant Health.* Shawnee Mission, KS: Author.

Scott, R. (2010, October). *The Transforming Power of Faith and Character.* Retrieved from http://www.lds.org/general-conference/2010/10/the-transforming-power-of-faith-and-character?lang=eng

Tracy, B. (2007). *Eat That Frog!: 21 Ways Great Ways to Stop Procrastinating and Get More Done in Less Time.* San Francisco, CA: Berrett-Koehler.

Tracy, B. (2010). *Goals!: How to Get Everything You Want – Faster Than You Ever Thought Possible* (2nd ed.). San Francisco, CA: Berrett-Koehler.

Williamson, M. (1992). *A Return to Love: Reflections on the Principles of A Course in Miracles.* New York, NY: Harper-Collins.

Ziglar, Z., & Ziglar, T. (2012). *Born to Win: Find Your Success Code.* Dallas, TX: SUCCESS Media.

ABOUT THE AUTHOR

Julie Connor, Ed.D., is a professional speaker, workshop facilitator, teacher, and consultant with more than thirty years of experience inspiring others to dream big, plan well, work smart, and transform their dreams into a course of action with tangible goals. Dr. Connor facilitates vision, mission, teamwork, collaboration, and goal-setting strategy training with adults and children, churches and schools, nonprofit organizations and businesses. She volunteers her time to provide workshops and training for at-risk youth and families. Dr. Connor also facilitates courageous conversations about multicultural inclusion and celebration of diversity. She lives in Overland Park, Kansas.

Julie invites you to discover your dream, define your purpose, maximize your talents, align your vision with your core values, and create your own action plan. Learn more at DrJulieConnor.com.

If you enjoyed this book, please consider leaving a great review on Amazon.com.

NOTES

_____
_____
_____
_____
_____
_____
_____
_____
_____
_____
_____
_____
_____
_____
_____
_____
_____
_____
_____
_____
_____
_____
_____
_____
_____
_____
_____
_____
_____
_____
_____
_____
_____
_____
_____

Dr. Julie Connor
LIGHT YOUR PASSION

NOTES